THE ANCIENT AND THE MODERN TEACHER OF POLITICS.

AN

INTRODUCTORY DISCOURSE

TO A

COURSE OF LECTURES

ON THE

STATE.

DELIVERED ON THE 10TH OF OCTOBER, 1859, IN THE LAW SCHOOL OF COLUMBIA COLLEGE.

BY

FRANCIS LIEBER,

PROFESSOR OF POLITICAL SCIENCE.

PUBLISHED BY THE BOARD OF TRUSTEES.

NEW YORK.

MDCCCLX.

DISCOURSE.

We are met together to discuss the State—that society which in infinite variety, from mere specks of social inception, to empires of large extent and long tradition, covers the whole earth wherever human beings have their habitation—that society which more than any other is identified, as cause and as effect, with the rise and fall of civilization—that society which, at this very period of mingled progress and relapse, of bravery and frivolity, occupies the mind of our whole advancing race, and which is the worthiest subject of contemplation for men, who do not merely adhere to instinctive liberty, but desire to be active and upright partakers of conscious civil freedom.

In the course of lectures which has been confided

to me, we shall inquire into the origin and necessity of the State and of its authority—is it a natural or an invented institution? into the ends and uses of government and into the functions of the State—is it a blessing or is it a wise contrivance, indeed, yet owing to man's sinful state as many fathers of the church considered all property to be; or is it a necessary evil, destined to cease when man shall be perfected? We shall inquire into the grandeur as well as into the shame of Political Man. We shall discuss the history of this, the greatest human institution, and ultimately take a survey of the literature appertaining to this enduring topic of civilized man.

This day I beg to make some preliminary remarks, chiefly intended to point out to you the position which, so far as I can discern, a public teacher of politics in this country and at this period, either occupies of necessity, or ought to occupy.

Antiquity differs from modern civilization by no characteristic more signally than by these two facts, that throughout the former there was but one leading state or country at any given period, while now several nations strive in the career of progress, abreast like the coursers of the Grecian chariot.

The idea of one leading nation, or of a "universal monarchy," has been revived, indeed, at several modern periods, and is even now proclaimed by those who know least of liberty, but it is an anachronism, barren in every thing except mischief, and always gotten up, in recent times, to subserve ambition or national conceit. It has ever proved ruinous, and Austria, France, and Spain have furnished us with commentaries.

The other distinctive fact is the recuperative energy of modern states. Ancient states did not possess it. Once declining, they declined with increasing rapidity until their ruin was complete. The parabola of a projectile might be called the symbol of ancient leading states—a curve, which slowly rises, reaches its maximum and precipitately descends, not to rise again, while the line of modern civilization, power, and even freedom, resembles, in several cases, those undulating curves which, having risen to one maximum, do not forego the rising to another, though they decline in the mean time to a minimum. Well may we call this curve the symbol of our public hope. If it were not so, must not many a modern man sink into the gloom of a Tacitus?

Now, closely connected with these, and especially with the second fact, it seems to me, is this observation, that in almost all the spheres of knowledge, action, or production, the philosophizing inquirer in antiquity makes his appearance when the period of high vitality has passed. The Greek and Roman grammarians inquired into their exquisite languages when the period of vigorous productiveness in them, of literary creativeness, was gone or fast going; when poets ceased to sing, historians ceased to gather, to compare and relate, and orators ceased to speak. The jurists collected, systematized, and tried to codify when a hale and energizing common law was giving rapidly way to the simple mandates and decrees of the ruler, or had ceased to be among the living and productive things; the æsthetic writer found the canons of the beautiful, when the sculptor and architect were stimulated more and more by imitation of the inspired masterworks created by the genius of by-gone days; and Aristotle founds the science of politics—we can hardly consider Pythagoras as the founder—when Athens and all Greece were drifting fast towards the breakers where the Roman wreckers were to gather the still glorious wrecks, while Cicero writes his work of the Republic when that dread time was approaching, in which, as a contemporary president of the French senate has officially expressed it, the Roman democracy ascended the throne in the person of the Cæsars—rulers, of whom we, speaking plain language, simply say that Tacitus and Suetonius have described them—people, whether we call them democracy or not, broken in spirit and so worthless that they rapidly ceased to know how to work for their living, or to fight for their existence —rulers and people whose history bears the impressive title, Decline and Fall of the Roman Empire. Or was, forsooth, the republican period of Rome, merely preparatory for the glorious empire, sold at auction by the prætorians?

It is different in modern times, thank God! Modern critics, philosophers, and teachers, in almost every branch, have lived while their age was productive, and frequently they have aided in bringing on fresh and sometimes greater epochs. In the science of politics this fact appears in a strong light. England has advanced in power, freedom, and civilization, since Thomas More, Harrington, Milton, Bacon, Sidney and Locke, William Temple, and even the latest of the last century, wrote and taught. France, whatever we may think of her present period of imperial transition and compressing absolutism, had far advanced beyond that state in which she was from the times of Bodinus and Montesquieu down to Rousseau or the Physiocrats, and will rise above the present period in which Guizot and De Tocqueville have given their works to her. Italy, however disappointed her patriots and friends may be at this moment, and however low that country, which is loved by our whole race, like a favorite sister of the family, had once sunk, stands forth more hopeful than, perhaps, she has done at any time since Thomas Aquinas* and Dante,† or Machiavelli, Paolo Sarpi, Vico, and all her writers down to Filangieri, that meditated on the State. If there are those who think that I have stated what is not warranted by the inadequate settlement of northern Italy—if, indeed, it prove a settlement—and by an arbitrary peace which, in its sudden conclusion, by two single men, unattended by any counsellor of their own, or representative of any ally, in behalf of near ninety millions of people, presents absolutism and foreign rule more nakedly

* De Rebus Publicis, et Principum Institutione Libri IV.

† De Monarchiâ.

than any other fact in modern Europe that I remember—if the affairs of Italy be viewed in this light, I must point to the fact that in spite of all this arbitrariness, the question: Do the people wish for this or that government, this or that dynasty? forces itself into hearing, and is allowed to enter as an element in the settlement of national affairs. It may indicate an imperfect state of things that this fact must be pointed out by the publicist as a signal step in advance; but it will be readily acknowledged as a characteristic change for the better, if we consider that in all those great settlements of the last century and of the present, by which the territories of the continental governments were rearranged, reigning houses were shifted, and states were made and unmade, Italy was consulted about herself no more than the princely hunter consults the hart which his huntsman cuts up for distribution among the guests and fellow-hunters. This century may yet see a united Italia, when at length it will cease to be *di dolor ostello* of that song of woe.

Germany, with whatever feeling he that loves her may behold that noble country, robbed as she is of her rightful heirship and historic adumbration as a nation in full political standing among the peoples of the earth, for her own safety and honor, and for European peace and civilization, has nevertheless advanced toward unity and freedom since the times of Grotius and Spinoza, (I call them hers,) and Puffendorff, Wolf, Schlötzer, and Kant, and will advance beyond what she is in these days of Zachariae, Welker, Mittermaier, and Mohl. Truth forces the philosopher to state the fact such as it is, although as patriot he finds it difficult to acknowledge the pittance of national political existence as yet doled out by modern history to that country, whose present intellectual influence vies with the political she once possessed under the Hohenstaufen.

The teacher of political science, in these days, without amusing himself with shallow optimism, has then the encouraging consciousness that his lot is not necessarily the mere summing up and putting on record, of a political life of better and of bygone days, never to return, not to be surpassed. The historian, whom Schlegel calls the prophet of the past, may in our days also be the sower of fresh harvests. The teaching of the publicist may become an element of living statesmanship; he may analyze essential fundamentals of his own society, of which it may not have been conscious, and the knowledge of which may influence future courses; he may awaken, he may warn and impress the lesson of inevitable historic sequences, and he may give the impulse to essential reforms; he may help to sober and recall intoxicated racers hurrying down on dangerous slopes, and he may assist the manly jurist and advocate, in planting on the outlying downs of civil life those hardy blades which worry back each aggressive wave, when walls of stone prove powerless against the stormy floods of invading power; he may contribute his share to the nautical almanac, and the sailing directions for the practical helmsman; he may pronounce truths which legislators quote as guiding rules in the parliament of his own country, or statesmen when met in a congress of entire nations; his teaching may modify, unconsciously to the actors themselves, and even in spite of their own belief, the course of passion, or set bounds to the worst of all political evils, public levity and popular indifference—if he will resolutely speak out the truth, and if he occupies a free position. Others must judge whether I am accustomed to do the one; I think I occupy the other.

Few public teachers of public law may have occupied a freer position than I do here before you. I belong to no party when teaching. All I acknowledge is PATRIA CARA, CARIOR LIBERTAS, VERITAS CARISSIMA. No government, no censor, no suspicious partisan watches my words; no party tradition fetters me; no connections force special pleading on me. I am surrounded by that tone of liberality, with that absence of petty inquisition which belong to populous and active cities, where the varied interests of life, religion, and knowledge, meet and modify one another. Those who have called me to this chair know what I have taught in my works, and that on no occasion have I bent to adjust my words to gain the approbation of prince or people. The trustees of this institution have called me hither with entire trust. Neither before nor after my appointment have they intimated to me, however indirectly, collectively or individually, by hint or question, or by showing me their own convictions, how they might wish me to tinge one or the other of the many delicate discussions belonging to my branches. I can gain no advantage by my teaching; neither title, order, or advancement on the one hand, nor party reward or political lucre on the other—not even popularity. Philosophy is not one of the high roads to the popular mind. All that the most gifted in my precise position could possibly attain to, is the reputation of a just, wise, fearless, profound, erudite, and fervent teacher. This, indeed, includes the highest reward which he who addresses you will endeavor to approach as near as lies within him.

But if the modern teacher of political science enjoys advantages over the teacher in ancient times, there are also difficulties which beset the modern teacher,—some peculiar to our own period, and some to our own country at this time.

Political science meets, to this day, with the stolid objection: What is it good for? Are statesmen made by books, or have the best books been made by the best statesmen? The name given to an entire party under Louis Philippe—the *doctrinaires*—seems to be significant in this point of view. You are, so we are told even by men of cultivated minds, not farther advanced than Aristotle was; and what must we think of the tree, if we judge by its fruits, the fantastic conceptions of the so-called Best State, with which the history of your science abounds? And Hume, the philosopher, said: "I am apt to entertain a suspicion that this world is still too young to fix any general truths in politics which will remain true to the latest posterity." But if the world is old enough to commit political sins and crimes of every variety, it cannot be too young to sink the shafts for the ore of knowledge, though the nuggets of pure truth may be rare. Does the miner of any other science hope for more?

Some friends have expressed their surprise that in my inaugural address I should have considered it necessary to dwell on the dignity and practical utility of political science as a branch of public instruction. I confess their surprise astonished me in turn. Not more than twenty years ago, Dahlmann said that "the majority of men believe to this day that every thing must be learned, only not politics, every case of which may be decided by the light of nature," meaning what is generally understood by common sense. Have things changed since these words were spoken? As late as in the year 1852, De Tocqueville, when presiding over the Academy of Morals and Politics, occupied himself in his annual address chiefly with the consideration of the prejudices still prevailing, not only among the people at large, but among statesmen and politicians themselves, against the science and studies cultivated by that division of the Institute of France;* and Hegel, esteemed by many the most profound and comprehensive thinker of modern times, says in his Philosophy of History, when speaking of that method of treating history which is called on the continent of Europe the pragmatic method, that "rulers, statesmen, and nations are wont to be emphatically commended to the teaching which experience offers in history. But what experience and history teach is this—that peoples and governments never have learned any thing from history or acted on principles deduced from it. Each period is involved in such peculiar circumstances, exhibits a condition of things so strictly idiosyncratic, that its conduct must be regulated by considerations connected with itself, and itself alone. Amid the pressure of great events, a general principle gives no hope. It is useless to revert to similar circumstances in the Past. The

* Even the minor lucubrations of this excellent writer have acquired an additional interest since death has put an end to his work. I would refer, therefore, to the National Intelligencer, Washington, 6th May, 1852, where the entire address alluded to is given.

pallid shades of memory struggle in vain with the life and freedom of the Present."

I have quoted this passage, which appears to me feeble and unphilosophical, for the purpose of showing that it is by no means useless to dwell, even in our age and in the midst of a civilized people, on the moral and practical importance, and not only on the scientific interest of the study of history and politics; and must dismiss, at least in this brief introductory lecture, a thorough discussion of these remarks—*inconsistent*, since their author admits one teaching of history and experience; *suicidal* to the philosopher, since they would extinguish the connection between the different "periods;" and what becomes of the connection of the events and facts within each period? What divides, philosophically speaking, the periods he refers to, so absolutely from one another? What becomes of continuity, without which it is irrational to speak of the philosophy of history?—*unhistorical*, for every earnest student knows how almost inconceivably great the influence of some political philosophers, and of the lessons of great historians, has been on the development of our race; *unreal*, since Hegel makes an intrinsic distinction between the motive powers of nations and states on the one hand, and of minor communities and individuals on the other; *destructive*, because what he says of political rules might be said of any rule of action, of laws, of constitutions; and *unpsychological*, because he ignores the connection between principle and practice, the preventive and modifying effect of the acknowledged principle or rule, whether established by experience, science, or authority, and its influence, in many cases, in spite of the actor, not unlike Julian the Apostate, whom Christianity did not wholly cease to influence, though he warred against it.

Was ever usurpation stopped in its career of passion by a moral or political apothegm? Possibly it was. The flashes of solemn truths sometimes cross the clouds of gathering crime and show how dark it is; but whether or not, is not now the question. Was ever burglar, crowbar in hand, stopped in his crime by reciting the eighth commandment? Probably not, although we actually know that murder, already unsheathed, has been sheathed again; but what is more important for the connected progress of our race is, that millions have been prevented from fairly entering on the path of filching or robbery, by receiving at home and in the school, the traditon of that rule, "Thou shalt not steal," and of the whole decalogue, as one of the ethical elements of their society, which acts, although unrecited, and even unthought of in a thousand cases, as the multiplication table or Euclid's Elements act, unrecited and unremembered at the time, in the calculations of the astronomer or of the carpenter, and in the quick disposition which military genius makes in the midst of confused battles, or a sea captain beating in dirty weather through a strait of coral reefs.

We Americans would be peculiarly ungrateful to political science and history, were we to deny their influence. Every one who has carefully studied our early history, and more especially our formative period, when the present constitution struggled into existence, knows how signally appear the effects of the political literature on which, in a great measure, the intellects of our patriots had been reared, and how often the measures which have given distinctness and feature to our system, were avowedly supported for adoption, by rules and examples drawn from the stores of history or political philosophy, either for commendation or warning. They had all fed on Algernon Sidney or Montesquieu; they had all read or scanned the history of the United States of the Netherlands, whence they borrowed even our name. It is the very opposite to what Hegel maintains, and the finding of these threads is one of the greatest delights of the philosophic mind.

Even if the science of politics were only, as so many mistake it to be, a collection of prescriptions for the art of ruling, and not quite as much of the art and science of obeying (why and when, whom and what, and how far we ought to obey)—but it is more than either—even then the science would be as necessary as the medical book is to the physician, or as the treatise on fencing, and the fencing master himself, are to him who wishes to become expert in the art. No rule merely learned by heart will help in complex cases of highest urgency, but the best decision is made by strong sense and genius that have been trained. It is thus in grammar and composition. It is thus in all spheres. Every one that we may call the practitioner, requires much that no book can give, but which will be of no use if not cultivated by teaching; or if it does not receive the opportunity of being brought into play, when natural gift, theory and its interpretation by experience melt into one homogeneous mass of choice Corinthian brass, in which the component elements can no longer be distinguished.

Although I shall not attempt to teach, in this course, actual statesmanship, or what has been styled the art of ruling, yet that which perhaps the older English writers more especially meant by the word Prudence, that is, foresight, (*prudentia futurorum*,) must necessarily enter as a prominent element in all political discussions; nor do I desire to pass on without guarding myself against the misconception that I consider the science, the Knowing, as the highest aim of man. As mere erudition stands to real knowledge, so does Knowing stand to Doing and Being. Action and character stand above science. Piety stands above theology; justice above jurisprudence; health and healing above medicine; poesy above poetics; freedom and good government above politics.

One of the most serious obstacles in the way of a ready reception of political science with that interest and favor which it deserves for the benefit of the whole community, is the confounding of the innumerable theories of the "Best State," and of all the Utopias, from Plato's Republic to modern communism, with political science. There is a suspicion lurking in the minds of many persons that the periods of political fanaticism through which our race has passed, have been the natural fruits of political speculation. But has the absence of political speculation led to no mischief, and not to greater ones? Let Asia answer. Our race is eminently a speculative race, and we had better speculate about nature, language, truth, the state, mind and man, calmly and earnestly, that is scientifically, than superstitiously and fanatically. One or the other our race will do. Brave jurists, noble historians, and free publicists, have, to say the least, accompanied the rising political movement of our race, with their meditations and speculations. The most sinister despots of modern times have been, and are to this day, the most avowed enemies of political science. Inquiry incommodes them; and although absolutism has had its keen and eloquent political philosophers, it is nevertheless true that the words embroidered on the fillet which graces the brow of our muse have ever been—In Tyrannos.

On the other hand, is there any period of intense action free from those caricatures by which the

Evil One always mocks that which is most sacred? Is theology, is medicine, are the fine arts, was the early period of Christianity, was the reformation, was ever a revolution, however righteous, was the revival of any great cause, the discovery of any great truth, free from its accompanying caricature? The differential calculus is a widely spread blessing to knowledge and our progress, yet it had its caricature in the belief of one of the greatest minds that it might be found a means to prove the immortality of the soul. The humanitarian, the theological and the political philosopher, know that the revival of letters and the love of Grecian literature mark a period most productive in our civilization, while the rise of modern national languages and literatures ushered in the new era, and has remained a permanent element of our whole advancement; yet Erasmus, the foremost scholar of his time, contemned the living speech of Europe, and allowed the dignity of language to none but the two idioms of antiquity. Our own age furnishes us with two notable instances of this historic caricature, appearing in the hall of history not unlike the grimacing monkey which the humorous architect of the middle ages sometimes placed in the foliage of his lofty architecture, near the high altar of the solemn cathedral. The history of labor, mechanical and predial, its gradual rise in dignity from the Roman slavery to its present union with science, is one of the golden threads in the texture we call the history of our race; yet we have witnessed, in our own times, the absurd effort of raising physical labor into an aristocracy as absolute, and more forbidding, than the aristocracy of the Golden Book of Venice, an absurdity which is certain to make its appearance again in some countries. Should we on that account, refuse to read clearly, and with delight, the rise of labor in the book of history? Should we deplore the gradual elevation of the woman peculiar to our race, and all that has been written to produce it, because in our age it has been distorted by folly, and even infamy, or by that caricature of courtesy which allows the blackest crime to go unpunished because the malefactor happens to be a female, thus depriving woman of the high attribute of responsibility, and, therefore, degrading her?

We honor science; we go further, we acknowledge that no nation can be great which does not honor intellectual greatness. Mediocrity is a bane, and a people that has no admiration but for victories gained on the battle-field, or for gains acquired in the market, must be content to abdicate its position among the leading nations. But no nation can be great that admires intellectual greatness alone, and does not hold rectitude, wisdom, and sterling character in public esteem. The list of brilliant despots, in government or science, always followed, as they are, by periods of collapse and ruin, is long indeed.

The faithful teacher of politics ought to be a manly and profound observer and construer. His business does not lie with fantastic theories or empty velleities, except to note them historically, and thus to make them instructive. Aristotle says, and Bacon quotes his saying approvingly, that the nature of a thing is best known by the study of its details, and Campanella, whom I quote only to remind you how early the truth was acknowledged, observes that a thing consists in its history, (its development), not in its momentary appearance, its phenomenon. Let us keep these two dicta before our eyes during our inquiries into the state, with this addition, that the knowledge of details yields fruitful acquisition only if it be gathered up in an ultimate knowledge of the pervading organism; and that, however true the position of Campanella, we must remember that politics is a moral science, and history, the record of political society, has not necessarily a prescribing character. Where this is forgotten men fall into the error of Symmachus pleading for Victoria, because the goddess of the forefathers, against the God of the Christians, because a new God; but where men forget the importance of history, development becomes impossible, and dwarfish schemes will set men in restless motion, like the insects of corruption busy in disintegrating mischief.

I neither belong to the school of those who, acknowledging free agency in the individual, teach, nevertheless, that nations follow a predestined fate, wholly independent of the beings composing them; nor do I belong to the modern optimists who complacently see nothing but advancement in our dubious age. I neither believe the region of the state to resemble the Olympus with its suspended ethics; nor do I belong to the retrospective school. I differ with those who follow Sismondi, a justly honored name, in the opinion that "every day must convince us more that the ancients understood liberty and the conditions of free government infinitely better than we do." The political progress of our race has been signal. How else can we explain these patent facts, that modern states with liberty have a far longer existence—where is the England of antiquity counting a thousand years from her Alfred, and still free?—that liberty and wealth in modern nations have advanced together, which the ancients considered axiomatically impossible; that modern liberty may not only advance with advancing civilization and culture, but requires them; that, occasionally at least, modern states pass through periods of lawlessness without succumbing, or that, as was mentioned before, modern societies have risen again after having passed through depressed periods threatening ultimate ruin; that in modern times alone, the problem has been solved, however rarely, of uniting progressive liberty with progressive order, which seemed to Tacitus a problem incapable of solution; that the moderns alone have shown the possibility of ruling large nations (not cities) with broadcast liberty; that in modern history alone we find civil liberty without enslaving the lower layer of society, and with the elimination of the idea of castes; that in modern societies alone essential and even radical changes in the political structure are effected without razing the whole edifice to the ground; that moderns alone have found the secret of limiting supreme public power, in whomsoever vested, by the representative principle and institutional liberty; that the moderns have discovered and developed the essential element of a lawful and loyal opposition, while the ancients knew only of political factions, not exchanging benches, but expelling or extirpating one another; that in modern times alone we meet with a fair penal trial, and with that august monument of civil liberty, a well-guarded trial for high treason; that the moderns have found the means of combining national vigor with the protection of individual rights; and that by international law a "system of states," as Europe has been called, can exist whose members are entire sovereign nations? Much of all this is owing to the spread and development of Christianity, and we moderns are very far from doing all we ought to do, but this does not prove Sismondi's opinion to be confirmed.

There are difficulties surrounding the teacher of politics, either exclusively belonging to our country, or at least presenting themselves here at present more decidedly. I ought not wholly to pass them over; for they show to what degree of indulgence a teacher is entitled; but I shall select a few only, and treat of them as briefly as may be.

I believe that the family of nations to which we belong, has arrived at a period in its political development in which the only choice lies between institutional and firmly established liberty, whether this be monarchical or republican as to the apex of the government, on the one hand; and on the other hand, intermittent revolution and despotism, or shifting anarchy and compression, which, like the surgeon's tourniquet, may stanch the blood for a moment, but has no healing power, nor can it be left permanently on the lacerated artery without causing mortification and death. Expanding institutional liberty alone is now conservative. There has been a conflict between freedom and despotism during the whole history of our race; but never before, it seems to me, have liberty with all its fervor, and absolutism, with all its imposing power or sepulchral sculpture, stood directly opposite to one another so boldly, and perhaps so grandly as at present. The advance of knowledge and intelligence gives to despotism a brilliancy, and the necessity of peace for exchange and industry, give it a facility to establish itself which it never possessed before. Although the political inquirer and reflecting historian know, as well as the naturalist, that life consists in the unceasing and reproductive pulsation—in the ever active principle of vitality, not in the few brilliant phenomena or in striking eruptions, yet radiant success always attracts admiration for the time being. Absolutism in our age is daringly draping itself in the mantle of liberty, both in Europe and here. What we suffer in this respect, is in many cases the after-pain of Rousseauism, which itself was nothing but democratic absolutism. There *is*, in our times, a hankering after absolutism, and a wide-spread, almost fanatical idolatry of Success, a worship of Will, whose prostrate devotees forget that will is an intensifier and multiplier of our dispositions, whatever they are applied to, most glorious or most abhorrent, as the case may be, and that will, without the shackles of conscience or the reins of a pure purpose, is almost sure of what contemporaries call Success. It is so easy to succeed without principle! It seems to me that those grave words in the solemn conclusion of De Tocqueville's Old Régime, have a far wider application at this time than the author gave to them. He says there that his countrymen are "more prone to worship chance, force, success, éclat, noise, than real glory; endowed with more heroism than virtue, more genius than common sense; better adapted for the conception of grand designs than the accomplishment of great enterprises." *

While thus political elements are jostling and preparing us for a greater struggle, it appears that in our times men are more bent than formerly on taking refuge in mere political formulas, such as universal suffrage and a despot, or universal suffrage and an absolute party. But wherever the people, fatigued by contest or disorder, go to sleep on a mere political formula, there political life and health

* I cannot dismiss this quotation without advising my younger friends to read, in connection with my remarks, the whole passage beginning with the words, "When I examine that nation." May they do it not only remembering that much that is said in it does not apply to the French alone, but also that De Tocqueville could say what he did say without being considered by the French unpatriotic. An American citizen could not have made similar remarks of the Americans without raising a storm of general indignation. No American student of political philosophy or history should be without that little volume, The Old Régime and the Revolution, by Alexis De Tocqueville, translated by John Bonner, New York, 1856.

and—may I call it so?—civil productiveness, rapidly decline and approach extinction, at the same time that those who still choose to act are arrayed against each other in all the bitterness which dogmatic formulas are apt to engender or to express.

To attract attention in the midst of these gusts of passion may not be an easy task. In addition I ought to mention with reference to our own country, three points—flattery, disrepute of politics, and a certain theory which has formed itself regarding the propriety of discussion.

The people of this country have been flattered so long by optimist speakers, lecturers, and authors, and the vice of exaggeration has become so common, that philosophic candor is felt by many as a lack of patriotic sympathy. The sovereign, the prince, as old writers used to call the power-holder, be he monarch or the people, likes courtiers, flatterers, and adulators, and he finds them. Truth becomes irksome, and while it is deemed heroic boldly to speak to a monarch, he who censures the sovereign in a republic is looked upon as no friend to the country.

Public affairs again have been frequently handled in such a manner and with such impunity that the word Politician has acquired a meaning which reminds us of the Athenian times, when philosophers thought it necessary to advise the seekers after truth to abstain from the agora. In former times the term Diplomatist was coupled with undesirable associations; the word Politician has now, in the minds of many, no enviable meaning. I do not conceal from myself that to me falls the duty of teaching the science of public affairs at a period of depressed public mind.

And lastly, it is a characteristic of our present public life that almost every conceivable question is drawn within the spheres of politics; when there, it is incontinently seized upon by political parties, and once within the grasp of parties, it is declared to be improper to be treated anywhere except in the arena of political strife. If it be treated elsewhere, in whatever spirit, it is taken for granted that the inquiry has been instituted for grovelling party purposes. Fair and frank discussion has thus become emasculated, and the people submit to dictation. There is a wide class of topics of high importance which cannot be taken in hand even by the most upright thinker without its being suspected that he is in the service of one party or section of the country and hostile to the other.

All this makes it—I do not say difficult to steer between the dangers; an attempt at doing this would be dishonest—but necessary to ask for a fair and patient hearing. No teacher can at any time dispense with that "favorable construction," for which the commons of England petition the ruler at the beginning of each parliament. An honest desire to hear truly what the speaker means is indispensable wherever human speech bridges over the cleft which separates individual from individual, but it becomes the more necessary, the more important the sphere of discussion is, and is granted the more scantily the more exciting the topic may be.

Montesquieu, in the preface of the Spirit of Laws, asks as a favor that a work of twenty years' labor may not be judged of by the reading of a moment, but that he may be judged by the whole. I too, placed in some respects more delicately than Montesquieu was, ask you to judge of the lectures which I am going to deliver by the whole and by the pervading spirit. My work is not, like Montesquieu's, a work of twenty years; it is more. Brief as this course will be, all I teach is the result of a long and checkered, an observing, and I hope a thoughtful life. Montesquieu, when he asks for the favor, adds: "I fear it will not be granted." I do not make this addition to my request. I simply speak to you as to friends, willing to hear what a man holds to be true and right in the region of political knowledge and action, the highest phase of which is civil freedom—a man who in his boyhood saw the flows and ebbs of the Napoleonic era and heard the European cry of oppression, and has from that great time to this longed or labored for liberty in speech and book, and in the teacher's chair, in prison and in freedom, well or wounded, in his native land and in his wedded country, and who feels that, as the one main idea through the whole life of him whom lately we have followed in our minds to his most honored grave, was the life of Nature with all her energies, so has been the leading idea and affection of him who speaks to you, from his early days to this hour, in spite of all the reverses and errors of our race, political justice, the life of civil freedom—liberty, not as a pleasing or even noble object to be pursued by classes freed from the oppressive demands of material existence, but as an element of essential civilization, as an earnest demand of self-respecting humanity, as an actuality and a principle of social life—as an evidence that we are created, not in the image of those beings that are below us, but of Him that is high above us.

www.ingramcontent.com/pod-product-compliance
Lightning Source LLC
LaVergne TN
LVHW011127110826
845150LV00008B/2269

* 9 7 8 1 4 1 8 1 9 5 4 3 4 *